Original title:
Wrapped in Christmas Wonder

Copyright © 2024 Creative Arts Management OÜ
All rights reserved.

Author: Evan Hawthorne
ISBN HARDBACK: 978-9916-90-950-8
ISBN PAPERBACK: 978-9916-90-951-5

A Carousel of Joyful Moments

Round and round the laughter flies,
Each silly face a sweet surprise.
We try to dance, but trip and fall,
Who knew that love could be so tall?

Spin the wheel, let's take a chance,
Wobble along, in this crazy dance.
A pie in the face, oh what a thrill,
Our cheeks are sore; can't get our fill!

The dog joins in, with wagging tail,
He barks and spins; without a fail.
Joy explodes like popcorn pop,
In this crazy ride, we never stop!

So hold my hand, don't let me fall,
We'll share the joy and have a ball.
With merry-go-rounds and big balloon,
Together we hum our happy tune.

Unfolding the Gifts of Togetherness

A pancake flop upon my head,
We laugh so hard, our giggles spread.
Syrup drips like honey rain,
Breakfast magic, what a gain!

In our fort made of blankets, high,
We plot to steal a cookie pie.
The cookie jar now stands in fear,
For little thieves are gathered near!

With poppers, balloons, and silly hats,
We dance like penguins, oh how that spats!
Jumping like frogs, we leap and shout,
In this wild fun, there's no doubt.

So here's to us, the goofy crew,
Making memories, just me and you.
Each moment a gift, sweet as can be,
Together forever, you and me!

Magical Journeys through Snow-Capped Tales

Snowflakes dance like tiny elves,
Making snowmen all by themselves.
Sleds go zooming down the hill,
Screams of laughter give us a thrill.

Hot cocoa spills on puffy coats,
While penguin slides steal all the motes.
Frosty breath and kids galore,
Winter fun we can't ignore.

Starlit Paths to Joyful Hearts

Under twinkling stars so bright,
Snowball fights bring pure delight.
Chasing shadows, running free,
Winter's magic, can't you see?

With cheeks so red and pants so wet,
In the snow, no room for regret.
Over hot chocolate, tales we weave,
Of joyful hearts that never leave.

The Scent of Pine and Cinnamon

Pine trees scent the frosty air,
While cinnamon wafts everywhere.
Cookies bake with slumps and drops,
As laughter overflows and pops.

Jingle bells and sugar highs,
Frosty windows, sweet surprise.
Candles flicker, warmth arrives,
In this season, joy thrives.

Portraits of Joy in Winter's Embrace

Snowmen wear the silliest hats,
Chasing dogs and sliding cats.
Kids in mittens, tumbling down,
Winter's laughter is the best sound.

Frosty noses, cheeks like cherries,
Winter stories, oh so merry.
All around, the joy expands,
In these portraits, laughter stands.

Laughter in the Snow

Snowflakes falling, soft and white,
Face plants happen, oh what a sight!
Hot cocoa mugs, laughter flows,
Sipping joy as the chilly wind blows.

Snowman smiles, with a carrot nose,
Chasing friends, oh how it goes!
Sledding down the hill with glee,
Falling flat, but so carefree.

Together Under Celestial Lights

Stars above, we make a wish,
Tripping over shoes, oh what a miss!
Holding hands, we dance around,
Tangled in laughter, lost and found.

Moonlight glows, a silver beam,
Fooling around, we laugh and scream!
A silly twirl, a goofy move,
In the dark, our hearts improve.

Illuminated Paths through the Cold

Flashlights flicker, shadows play,
Bumping into trees, we lose our way!
Giggles echo in frosty air,
Chasing snowballs, oh, beware!

Cold is biting, but spirits high,
Running wild, beneath the sky.
Trips and tumbles, we laugh out loud,
Best buddies, feeling proud.

The Heart's Warmest Embrace

A warm hug shared, the chill retreats,
With silly jokes, our rhythm beats.
Snuggled close by the crackling fire,
Failing attempts at a hotdog spire.

Spilled popcorn making quite a mess,
But in this moment, who'd want less?
Laughter's chorus, pure delight,
In our cozy, glowing night.

Festival of Glows and Delight

In the park with my bright lantern,
I tripped over a tiny fern,
The giggles echoed through the night,
Who knew a plant could cause such fright?

Cotton candy clouds up high,
Sprinkling sugar from the sky,
My friend just fell into the pie,
Now he's stuck and wants to cry!

Fireworks went boom, oh dear,
But someone mistook it for a beer,
They yelled, 'Watch out!', but it was too late,
And now we're dodging confetti fate!

With smiles that wrapped us tight,
We danced in pure delight,
The festival lights wink and glower,
As laughter blooms like a radiant flower.

A Celebration of Twinkling Dreams

Stars are winking in the night,
I'm sure they've had a drink too bright,
A dreamer's dance begins to sway,
With flip-flops in the Milky Way!

The moon is wearing shades so cool,
While squirrels have taken over the pool,
We float on clouds and sip sweet tea,
In a land where cats can finally flea!

Giggles bounce from dream to dream,
As jellybeans spill from every seam,
We all declared, 'Let's trap a sun!'
And then we realized we'd just begun!

The spirit of dreams, it whirls and spins,
In this celebration, everyone wins,
So come and join the happy team,
And let's wake up from this wild dream!

The Spirit of Togetherness

Here we gather, snacks in hand,
To build a castle, look so grand,
But the dog thinks it's a game to play,
He jumps right in, then runs away!

Neighbors sharing their best dish,
Someone's salad turns into a swish,
A flying carrot meets a shoe,
Now we cheese of our joy anew!

We sing a song, but out of tune,
As cats join in—oh what a swoon!
With laughter ringing through the night,
Together we spark true delight!

Grandpa jokes, they rule the place,
While all pretend to hide their face,
So here's to bonds that never break,
In every smile, our hearts awake!

Sweet Nostalgia of December

Snowflakes dance in cozy air,
With cocoa spilling everywhere,
I take a sip and burn my tongue,
Maybe winter's just too young!

The tree is up, lights tangle tight,
As my cat pounces, oh what a sight,
I try to decorate, what a twist,
Now we own the world's weirdest list!

Old songs play, and we all sing,
Off-key bells start to ring,
Ghosts of Christmas past are near,
Offering cookies, love, and cheer!

So here's to laughter on cold, bright nights,
To sweet nostalgia in joyous flights,
May every moment freeze in place,
As smiles light up each friendly face!

The Dance of Snowflakes and Stars

Snowflakes twirl like ballerinas,
With grace that leaves them breathless.
Stars wink in their chilly laughter,
While winter wonders, 'Who's the best?'

They swirl and glide in cosmic play,
Creating chaos in the night.
One flake trips, 'Hey, not today!'
The star chuckles, 'What a sight!'

Each star claims they're the hundredth,
Snowflakes blush, oh, such a show!
With frosty twirls, they spark and spin,
In a mad dance, they come and go.

A final bow, a cold wind sighs,
They scatter 'til next winter night.
But in our hearts and hopeful skies,
Their dance remains, pure frozen light.

Kindled Fires and Shared Smiles

Around the fire, stories fly,
Each laugh pops like a cozy flame.
We share our secrets, woes, and pies,
And joke about the 'who's to blame?'

The marshmallows toast, then drop,
Into the flames, a sticky mess.
We giggle as the sad ones plop,
Burnt offerings of sugar stress.

With sipping cocoa, we begin,
To recite the tales of old.
Of heroes brave, who always win,
But mostly about grandma's mold.

As embers glow, we feel the cheer,
A warmth that spreads, not just from heat.
Kindled fires and smiles so near,
Where laughter and friendship meet.

Tales of Generosity and Kindness

In the town where kindness bloomed,
People shared more than their treats.
A neighbor gave a cat costume,
To unsuspecting, grumpy Pete.

They laughed and danced, a sight to see,
While Pete grumbled, 'What's the fuss?'
But he wore it, with heartfelt glee,
Cried out, 'Bring on the festive bus!'

A dinner served to those in need,
With seconds and thirds to spare.
Generosity planted the seed,
And kindness grew like fresh garden hair.

With silly acts, and pies that fly,
Let's sprinkle joy with every deed.
For in a world where kindness lies,
We all can bloom, sow love's good seed.

Joys Unfolding in the Frost

In the frost, the world's aglow,
With sparkly sights, like a dream.
We slip and slide, 'Oh no! Oh no!'
And laugh 'til we fall into the cream.

The trees wear coats of icy lace,
While snowmen flaunt their bumpy hats.
With frozen noses, we embrace,
As snowballs fly like friendly bats.

We sip hot tea, wrapped in blankets,
And tell tales of slips and trips.
Embracing every chilly "Thanks!"
As frost nips at our toes and lips.

The magic stirs, breath forms a cloud,
As children shout with all their might.
In joys unfolding, we are proud,
To dance in winter's chilly light.

Beneath the Glittering Stars

Beneath the stars, we shared a snack,
A sandwich fell—my dog was quick!
He gobbled it with such a knack,
Now thinks he's a gourmet pick!

We laughed so hard, we lost our breath,
Trying to trap the twinkling lights,
But tripping over roots, I met my death,
With crickets as my laughter's heights.

The constellations, wise and bright,
Giggled softly at our clumsiness,
As we chased our shadows in the night,
And stumbled into a patch of mess.

Next time, I'll bring a proper meal,
No secrets hiding in my pack—
Unless, of course, it's quite the deal,
And let my pup have his heart attack!

The Magic of Evergreen Dreams

In a forest dense with evergreen,
I lost my way, but found a snack,
A cookie jar was quite the scene,
Until a squirrel launched an attack!

The critter stole my treat with flair,
It darted up a tree to gloat,
Its tiny paws held high in air,
While I just stood, an empty coat.

I yelled, 'Hey, you! That was my lunch!'
But it just chattered in delight,
I guess my dreams, in fact, got crushed,
By fluffy robbers of the night.

So now I carry treats for two,
And share my snacks with all the fur,
For magic lies in sharing too,
And maybe I'll teach them to purr!

Frosted Memories in the Twilight

In twilight's glow, I tried to skate,
But slipped right into snow so deep,
With frosted hands, I found my fate,
An awkward tumble, oh so sweet!

My friends all laughed, they wouldn't stop,
As I became a snowman, dude,
Trying to rise, I'd slip and flop,
With snowflakes dancing, oh so rude!

The chilly air was filled with cheer,
As hot cocoa awaited back,
I dreamed of warmth, forget my fear,
While snowmen danced, holding my snack.

Next winter's tale, I plan to win,
With better skates and maybe skills,
But in my heart, I know within,
That laughter's worth the winter chills!

An Evergreen Embrace

Amidst the pines, I took a stroll,
When suddenly, I lost my shoe,
The trees all giggled, played their role,
As squirrels danced around me too.

I searched for ages, it was absurd,
While laughing birds mocked my plight,
But then I saw a lovely herd,
Of deer, who joined in my delight.

They pranced and danced, then found my gear,
A shoe returned with deerish grace,
I laughed so hard, I shed a tear,
A forest party, my happy place.

Now every walk is filled with cheer,
As I indulge in nature's play,
For magic blooms when friends are near,
With evergreen hugs, we greet the day!

Midnight Wishes on Silent Nights

In the dead of night, I creep around,
Whispering wishes, without a sound.
I wish for snacks, not a care in sight,
Only to find crumbs, what a fright!

The stars above wink, oh so sly,
While I trip over toys, oh my, oh my!
Midnight snacks turn into a feast,
But soon I hear the cat, at least!

A mouse in the corner, plotting my fall,
While I munch away, I'll have a ball.
The moon giggles, casting a glow,
As I search for more snacks, row by row!

By dawn, I'll regret this savory spree,
With a tummy that's larger than a tree.
But every midnight wish contains a cheer,
For dreams taste sweeter when snacks are near!

Glittering Paths of Hope

I walked a path that glittered bright,
Thought I lost my way, but what a sight!
A trail of donuts, frosted and round,
Leading me where joy can be found!

With sprinkles on top, who could resist?
I paused for a second, couldn't be missed.
Stars in the sky, they twinkled in rush,
While I devoured pastries with a crush!

But then I tripped on a rogue cupcake,
And landed undignified with a shake.
So much for grace on this glittering lane,
Now I'm sticky, covered in icing and grain!

Yet here comes a dog, with a wag and a bark,
He thinks I'm the best, brightening the dark.
So I laugh with delight, despite the cake stain,
On this sparkling path, I'm perfectly sane!

Embraced by the Chill of Hope

The winter air bites as I bundle tight,
Chasing away frost, with all of my might.
Hot cocoa flows like a river of cheer,
While fluffy marshmallows disappear!

The snowflakes dance, like they're on a spree,
Whispering secrets, just for me.
I step on a patch, hear a loud crunch,
Squirrels laugh from their frosty brunch!

I build a snowman, round as a ball,
He looks quite dapper, but what if he falls?
An avalanche looms, oh what a fright,
But I can't stop laughing in the bright moonlight!

So I sip my drink, while snowflakes descend,
With laughter and joy, on that I depend.
Chilled to the bone, but warmed from within,
In winter's dream, let the fun begin!

A Symphony of Seasons' Magic

In springtime, flowers dance with glee,
But my allergies sing the blues for me.
Bees buzz around, they're busy and bold,
While I sneeze and cough, feeling quite old!

Summer arrives, the sun turns up high,
I jump in the pool, but oh, how I fly!
Slipped on a floatie, what a grand splash,
Now there's water everywhere—what a crash!

Autumn's colors, a dazzling show,
Pumpkin spice lattes, all in a row.
Yet my pumpkins are attacked by a squirrel,
As I chase him away, we make quite the whirl!

Winter wraps all in a fuzzy embrace,
But I slip on the ice, what a disgrace!
Seasons may change, and I might fall flat,
But laughter stays with me, that's where it's at!

Woven Wishes of the Heart

I wished on a star, it winked at me,
Told me my dreams were free as a bee.
I asked for a sandwich, but got a shoe,
Now I'm munching on laces, oh what to do!

My heart's full of wishes, each one a clown,
Twirling and dancing, wearing a frown.
They trip on my hopes, they fall on their face,
Laughing at dreams like they're some kind of race.

When I weave my wishes, I grab some thread,
Stitching together what's stuck in my head.
A blanket of giggles, a patchwork of fun,
Wrap me up tight till the day is done.

So if you see wishes just floating around,
They might be the dreams that I've accidentally found.
Grab them and hold them, make them your own,
And share in the laughter, we'll never be alone!

Flickering Flame of Holiday Hope

The candles are flickering, one starts to dance,
My cat is suspicious, thinks it's a chance.
To pounce and to play with the light on the wall,
I shout, "No candle! Let's not have a brawl!"

The cookies are burning, oh what a sight,
But Santa won't mind if they taste just right.
I'll frost them with laughter, some sprinkles of cheer,
And hope that the reindeer won't shed any tears.

The tree is all tangled, those lights are a mess,
Each time I fix it, I love it, I guess.
But then it blinks twice, like it's part of a show,
I check if it's Christmas or just a disco!

So here's to the holidays, bright and bizarre,
With mishaps and giggles that shine like a star.
Let's twist and let twirl through the festive parade,
With flickering flames that surely won't fade!

Chasing Snowflakes in Dreamland

In dreamland I run where the snowflakes play,
They tickle my nose and then melt all away.
I try catching magic, but it slips through my hands,
Like hugs from a llama in polka dot bands.

The snowmen are giggling, their noses all bright,
One wobbles and falls, what a comical sight!
They throw snowballs at me, but they're pillows of fluff,
Oh no, my defenses—these snowflakes are tough!

We've built a fort made of frosty delight,
With walls made of giggles, oh what a night!
But then comes a snowstorm, full of cheer and chaos,
We're dancing and spinning—oh, what a pathos!

So let's chase the snowflakes, those beautiful sprites,
And laugh through the nights, till we get into fights.
In dreamland we'll linger, where winter is grand,
Embracing the joy—holding snowflake in hand!

Embracing the Spirit of Giving

I wrapped up my worries with a big sturdy bow,
Gave them to others, they're dancing in tow.
They giggled and jiggled, they spun like a top,
Now everyone's laughing, we just cannot stop!

I found a lost sock and a stray paperclip,
Added a cookie, now that's quite a trip!
I packaged my kindness in a glittery crate,
So now when you open it, don't hesitate!

The spirit of giving is silly and bright,
It sneaks up like shadows in the depth of the night.
A hug here, a smile there, what could it cost?
In the treasure of joy, you'll never be lost!

So share all your jokes, your dances, your cheer,
Embrace every giggle, grab hold of it dear.
For when we are giving, we're spinning around,
In the circle of laughter, true joy can be found!

A Bowl of Cheer and Unity

Gather round the table, please,
With bowls of soup and cheesy peas.
Laughter fills the air so bright,
As we debate the wrong and right.

Uncle Joe brings his special stew,
That smells like old, forgotten shoe.
But we taste it with a grin so wide,
Though for the bathroom, we may need a guide.

Let's raise our spoons, let's share a laugh,
At auntie's dance, it's quite the gaffe.
Together we munch and sip with glee,
In this bowl of love, just you and me.

So here's to joy, both near and far,
In every bite, we're dining stars.
Unity's spice, the secret blend,
A bowl of cheer that has no end.

Stories Kindled by Holiday Flames

Gather 'round the fire so warm,
Where stories grow and friendships swarm.
A holiday tale with a twist or two,
About a turkey that once flew.

Grandpa swears he saw it soar,
Right over Aunt Sue's front door.
She chased it down with stuffing fast,
But the turkey's luck was unsurpassed.

Then there's the cat who stole the scene,
With tinsel braids and a Christmas dream.
Caught in the act of a glitter spree,
Now the tree's a feline selfie!

So toast those tales, let laughter rise,
With flickering flames beneath the skies.
Each chuckle spins our memories bright,
As we sit and revel in pure delight.

The Journey of the Heart

Oh, the journey of love, what a ride,
From awkward dates to a joyful slide.
With hearts a-flutter and giddy thrills,
We navigate love's many hills.

Met at the café, our fates aligned,
Shared a croissant, our hearts entwined.
But spilled my drink all over your shoes,
You laughed so hard, I couldn't refuse.

Then there were roses, which turned to weeds,
You said, "Love grows, just mind the seeds!"
Through ups and downs, we danced and twirled,
In this comical journey, love unfurled.

With every bump, a giggle grows,
In the garden of love, we watch it bloom.
Through thick and thin, we trip and fall,
In this strange journey, we've answered the call.

Glimmers of Joy through the Frost

In winter's chill, we bundle tight,
With rosy cheeks, a merry sight.
Snowflakes dance, like tiny fuss,
As we sip cocoa on the bus.

Oh, how the snowmen stand so proud,
With carrot noses, they draw a crowd.
Frosty smiles, with scarf and hat,
And one cheeky bird that flies in flat.

We slip and slide on icy streets,
Sharing giggles with chilly beats.
Snowball fights and laughter loud,
Joy shines through the winter shroud.

So here's to frosty, fun-filled days,
With glimmers of joy in snowy ways.
We'll laugh and cheer 'til springtime shows,
In this winter wonderland of giggles and snow.

Echoes of the Season's Joy

The snowmen stand, looking quite stout,
With buttons asking, 'What's this fuss about?'
Children giggle—it's all a big game,
While parents sip cocoa, and somehow feel fame.

In scarves that are bright, they dance 'round the park,
With snowflakes like sprinkles that land on a lark.
Mittens mismatched, yet fashion's a breeze,
Who knew winter could come with a side of unease?

The holiday tunes, they echo and glow,
With crazy reindeer putting on quite a show.
The fruitcake's a prize, it's bathed in despair,
But that's how we know that the season is fair!

So raise up your mugs, let's clink and rejoice,
For laughter and cheer, they're the best kind of choice.
In echoes of joy, let's make merry noise,
Who knew winter would come with such fun-loving poise?

A Canvas of Snowflakes and Wishes

The sky drops white confetti with flair,
A canvas of snowflakes, floating in air.
Each flake is unique, like a witty remark,
They tickle your nose, leaving trails that embark.

Kids craft their visions, like artists at play,
With snowballs in hand, and laughter on display.
The dog joins the fun, with a leap and a bark,
He thinks it's a game, just a walk in the park.

But wait, what's this? The cat's watching close,
In her tiny warm sweater, she thinks she's the host.
She pounces on snow, with a delicate grace,
But one slip on ice sends her off in a chase!

With hot cocoa hugs and cookies to share,
Let's gather 'round warmth, showing love and good care.
For each snowflake whispers a wish as it lands,
Here's to laughter and joy, let's make snowy plans!

Twinkling Eyes Amidst the Cheers

With twinkling eyes beneath winter's spell,
The townsfolk gather, oh boy, what a swell!
In hats that are silly, each style a surprise,
You'd think they were elves, with their giggles and sighs.

The lights strung with care, like stars made of cheer,
Bring warmth to the heart, as we sing loud and clear.
The tree stands so grand, looking proud and aglow,
While the squirrels roll their eyes, saying, 'Give us a show!'

Plates piled high with treats, a buffet so wide,
We munch on the goodies, and let laughter collide.
The punch bowl is wobbly, like dad after ten,
'These cookies are healthy!' he'll say, then eat ten.

So here's to the cheers, and the fun that we share,
To goofy traditions, and snow in our hair!
Let's dance in the moonlight, while all the stars beam,
With twinkling eyes bright, we'll savor the dream!

Silver Linings of Frosty Mornings

The frost paints the windows, a glittering scene,
As children dream big, wearing pajamas so green.
They hop from their beds with a leap and a shout,
'Look mom, it's magic, come see what's about!'

Outside, the world sparkles, like diamonds all spread,
But where's all the warmth? Oh dear, it fled!
With noses all pink, they bundle and trod,
Each step is a dance, oh, how they applaud!

Yet grandma, with wisdom, says, 'Breathe in the air,
This chill is a blessing, let kindness declare!'
So they build little forts, with laughter and glee,
While pretending to rule, on their throne made of brie.

With cocoa in hand and whipped cream as crowns,
They toast to the winter, in colorful gowns.
As silver linings glimmer, troubles disappear,
In frosty mornings, there's magic, my dear!

Whispers of Frosted Dreams

In the frosty air, we sing,
All the joys the snow can bring.
But my nose is frozen stiff,
As I chase an errant whiff.

Snowflakes dance upon my hat,
While I chase a playful cat.
It pounces, then takes a dive,
I'm just glad I'm still alive!

Hot cocoa spills on my shoe,
As I try to sip and chew.
Marshmallows float, all so grand,
But now I'm losing my stand.

Frosted dreams of sugar high,
Santa's sleigh passes by.
With laughter ringing so clear,
Let's hope my socks won't disappear!

Tinsel Glow and Yuletide Bliss

Tinsel wrapped around the tree,
Looks quite lovely, don't you see?
But every time I walk by,
I catch my sweater—oh my my!

Cookies baked but burnt on ends,
Love is thick with all my friends.
We gather 'round with so much glee,
Who knew a pie could bite back me?

Gifts are hiding, wrapped with flair,
Yet I smell my dog's foul hair.
As he chews my twinkling lights,
I'm just thankful for the fights.

Into the night, we'll sing our songs,
Dancing silly, righting wrongs.
In this tinsel glow we find,
Yuletide bliss and peace of mind!

Gleam of Evergreen Enchantment

In a forest deep and wide,
An evergreen takes it in stride.
Dressed in baubles, looking fine,
But what's that? Some squirrels align!

They're planning heists of ornaments,
Swiping all that makes sense tense.
One stole a star and ran so fast,
Now we're left with a laugh, alas!

The lights are tangled in a mess,
I must confess, I guess, I guess.
As I wrestle with the strands,
Sister's rolling on the sands.

But with each giggle and cheer,
The season's magic feels so near.
In the gleam of festive fun,
Joy unravels, we've all won!

A Hearthside Tale of Joy

By the hearth, with flames aglow,
Stories spill, and laughter flows.
Grandpa's tales of snowball fights,
End in giggles through the nights.

Marshmallows toast with sticky glee,
But oh dear! Not yet for me!
The cat jumps up, a sly little thief,
Replacing my snack with disbelief.

Cookies vanish, and then I spy,
A trail of crumbs that waves bye-bye.
Unruly pets and sibling sprawls,
All join in for the evening calls.

With heart and warmth, we'll raise a cheer,
To the joys of this festive year.
In hearthside tales, our spirits soar,
Together, we'll laugh forevermore!

Embracing the Season's Magic

The snowflakes dance, a wiggly troupe,
As the kids all bounce, in their puffy loop.
Hot cocoa spills, a chocolatey mess,
Mom sighs, but she knows it's just winter's stress.

The trees wear coats, all sparkling and bright,
Neighbors argue 'bout who's got the best light.
Sledding down hills, oh what a delight,
While falling on faces feels perfectly right.

Socks from the dryer, all mismatched and fun,
Who knew this chaos could be number one?
As winter giggles, we all find our cheer,
Embracing the season, oh how it's dear!

With snowman armies, and carrot nose fights,
We gather together, sharing our plights.
These wintery moments, they come and they go,
But laughter rings out, it's the best kind of glow.

A Journey Through Winter's Embrace

Winter arrives, with a shiver and shake,
The snowman's built, oh what a mistake!
His nose a good carrot, but his smile's a bit sad,
He cries out for warmth, oh this winter's so bad!

The squirrels are playing, in jackets so small,
While robins look lost, should they even call?
A journey through winter, oh where do we roam?
With hot hands so frozen, we yearn for a home.

We bake up some cookies that stick to the pan,
Then giggle and laugh at our baking plan.
But through all the chaos, the slips and the slides,
Winter's embrace is where laughter resides.

With layers so thick, we waddle like ducks,
The ice on the pond gives a few gentle bucks.
But joy rides alongside, as we stumble and grin,
In winter's embrace, the fun's found within.

Holiday Whispers

Holiday whispers, they tickle the air,
With fruitcake disasters and strings of despair.
A cat on the tree, now that's a surprise,
As ornaments tumble, everyone cries!

The lights start to twinkle, then decide to go out,
We dig through the attic with a cry and a shout.
As granddad tries fixing the mess we have made,
We wonder if hot glue's the fix for our trade!

Wrapping up presents, and losing the tape,
A gift full of socks turns out to escape.
But as we all gather, together we blend,
The holiday whispers form fun without end.

From cookies to chaos, and laughter galore,
These moments of joy are what we adore.
In all of the mayhem, our hearts sing so bright,
Holiday whispers, take wing in the night.

A Tapestry of Frost and Light

A tapestry woven with frost and with cheer,
The chill in the air, but the smiles are near.
As mittens get lost, the kids start to sing,
With snowflakes like diamonds, what joy they bring!

The shovels are out, the sidewalks a mess,
But laughter erupts, it's all part of the test.
While snowball fights break, and giggles abound,
Winter's sweet chaos wraps tightly around.

With parties and potlucks, we tackle the night,
With folks dressed as snowmen, oh what a sight!
From cheesy old sweaters to reindeer galore,
This tapestry glimmers, who could ask for more?

So let's frolic through winter, and cherish the freeze,
In this tapestry's chaos, we'll do as we please.
For in every cold day, and in every snow's flight,
Lies the warmth of our friendships, both cozy and bright.

Nostalgic Glimmers of the Season

Snowflakes dance in a silly way,
But land on noses where they stay.
Hot cocoa spills from my cup,
While my cat thinks he's in a hiccup.

Trees are decked with shining lights,
While the dog's tangled in festive sights.
Grandma's cookies smell divine,
Until I find out that they're mine!

The carolers sing, but off-key,
My neighbor nods with glee and a plea.
The ugly sweaters come out to play,
Worn proudly on this holiday.

Laughter echoes through the frost,
In the merry mayhem, no one's lost.
These moments glimmer, oh so bright,
In the chaos, we find delight.

An Ode to Comfort and Kindness

Here's to the socks, mismatched and warm,
And blankets that hug like a gentle charm.
When friends drop by, it's a riot,
Over pizza that looks like a science diet.

A fuzzy sweater from days of yore,
With stains that tell stories and more.
We laugh and share, our hearts aligned,
With every gesture, kindness defined.

The tea kettle whistles with glee and cheer,
As stories spill over, we hold them dear.
In a world that's full of piles and glitz,
It's comfort we crave, not just the bits.

So raise a glass filled with old fruit punch,
To kindness that warms us, it's the best lunch.
In this crazy life, let's all be kind,
With laughter and love, our fates intertwined.

The Rhythm of Heartfelt Celebration

Drums beat softly, a joyful sound,
As we gather round, the fun is profound.
With hats on heads and smiles so wide,
We celebrate life with friends by our side.

The dance floor's waiting for moves quite wild,
As Grandma spins like an excited child.
We clink our cups filled with fizzy cheer,
In moments like these, we shed every fear.

Balloons pop and confetti flies high,
As cake meets face, oh what a sly pie!
Laughter erupts like a joyous song,
In this merry chaos, we all belong.

So let's toast to moments that make time freeze,
With rhythm and joy, we find our ease.
In each heartfelt laugh, a treasure resides,
As life's party rolls on, like endless tides.

Stories Shared by the Fireside

Gather 'round, the flames flicker bright,
With shadows dancing in the dim light.
A tale unfolds, with suspense and cheer,
Where marshmallows roast and memories appear.

The ghost of Aunt Margie with a wild hairdo,
Tells stories of when she met a shoe.
"Why did the chicken cross the road?"
The punchline erupts, we lift the abode!

The crackle of wood gives a soft embrace,
While everyone laughs at the silliest face.
With mugs of hot cocoa and giggles galore,
These moments together, we all do adore.

So here's to firesides, crackling and warm,
Where stories are shared, in every form.
As long as we gather, with laughter to spare,
These tales will live on, we're always aware.

Lullabies Beneath Twinkling Lights

Twinkling stars dance all night,
A baby needs to sleep tight.
But the cat thinks it's a game,
Pouncing around, it's quite the fame.

Crickets chirp a silly tune,
While the dog howls at the moon.
Mom's trying hard not to yawn,
As little Timmy dreams of dawn.

Chasing shadows, making sound,
Lullabies can't be found.
Yet tired eyes refuse to close,
As the nightingale loudly dozes.

So sleep sweetly, dear little mite,
Tomorrow brings more playful sights.
With a wink from the moon's glow,
Goodnight, it's time for dreams to flow.

Frost-Kissed Memories of Home

Snowflakes fall like silly hats,
As we chase slippery cats.
Grandma's cookies burn in a blaze,
All of us caught in a sugary haze.

The fireplace pops with delight,
While the kids start a snowball fight.
Dad slips down with a bumbling cheer,
And the dog goes chasing, oh dear!

We build a snowman, round and wide,
With a carrot nose and arms quite spry.
But he tips over, what a scene!
And now we're left with a chilly bean!

Hot cocoa spills, oh such a plight!
But laughter keeps our hearts warm at night.
Frost-kissed memories linger dear,
In a home filled with giggles and cheer.

A Canvas of Silver and Gold

A painter's dream in hues so bright,
With a brush that wiggles with delight.
Silver fish swim in a sea of spray,
While goldfish munch on a cupcake array.

The canvas giggles, what a sight,
As colors crash, a colorful fight.
A purple cow jumps over the moon,
While dancing llamas hum a tune.

Pigs in tutus swirl around,
In this land of laughter found.
As paint spills like silly confetti,
Creating a scene of chaos, yet pretty!

So grab your spatula, mix it all,
Let your imagination fly and sprawl.
A canvas of silver and gold awaits,
Where laughter meets art and creates.

Tales from an Evergreen Forest

In a forest, ever so green,
Where squirrels hold a daily routine.
They gather nuts, quite the spree,
While the owls laugh, 'Oh, can't you see?'

A bear tries to dance, oh so bold,
But trips on a log, landing in old mold.
The rabbits chuckle, rolling in glee,
As the trees sway, singing a spree.

Mice tell tales of cheese and delight,
While porcupines sparkle under moonlight.
Every corner, a giggle to hear,
In this forest filled with cheer.

So venture in, take a peek inside,
Where laughter roams, and dreams collide.
Tales from the forest, wild and free,
Bringing smiles, just wait and see!

A Feast of Warmth and Togetherness

Gather 'round the table, oh so wide,
With mashed potatoes cooked with pride.
The turkey's dry, but we'll all pretend,
And pass the gravy 'til the very end.

Aunts are arguing about the pie,
Uncle Fred just let out a sigh.
Laughter bounces like a bouncing bean,
In this festive scene, where chaos is keen.

Cousins wrestling in a food fight spree,
Mom rolls her eyes, 'Oh dear, not me!'
But it's all in fun, no need for remorse,
We'll just blame it on the mashed potato course.

So here's to the mess of this holiday feast,
With friends and family, we love the least.
The warmth of togetherness fills the air,
Even if Uncle Joe forgot to comb his hair.

Carols Echo through the Night

Singing carols in the freezing cold,
Voices crack, but we feel bold.
Frosty noses and frozen toes,
Is that a snowman? No, just my clothes!

Jingle bells and off-key notes,
We harmonize like a bunch of goats.
Neighbors peek out, rolling their eyes,
While we belt tunes under the winter skies.

Mittens stuck on the wrong hands,
But no one cares; this chaos stands.
Hot cocoa spills on the front porch floor,
And just like that, we start to sing more.

So let the laughter and music ring,
Even if we can't hold a tune or sing.
For in this night, so merry and bright,
We'll keep caroling till the morning light.

The Gleam of Hope and Harmony

Lights twinkle like stars in the sky,
A glow in the heart, no need to be shy.
With cookies and cocoa, we toast to cheer,
As laughter whispers, 'The holidays are here!'

The holiday cheer can get a bit wild,
Like kids on sugar, bright-eyed and smiled.
But in the chaos, hope takes its seat,
Gathering with joy, we can't be beat.

Fires crackle, warmth fills the air,
Family and friends are everywhere.
A tinsel tornado, we hang on tight,
With love and giggles, we'll savor the night.

So share in the moments, sweet and bright,
For in this season, let's delight.
With harmony ringing, and spirits so high,
May laughter and kindness always reply.

Holiday Dreams Wrapped in Light

Presents piled high, a mountain of glee,
But 'Do Not Open' stares right back at me.
Twirling around the tree, I feel like a sprite,
With dreams wrapped in paper, oh what a sight!

Elves in the kitchen, baking away,
While the cookies go missing, it's child's play.
Ribbons and bows tangled tight as can be,
Trying to wrap gifts with no one to see.

But wait! There's a cat in the Christmas tree,
Who knew they liked climbing so much, oh gee!
As ornaments scatter across the floor,
All my hard work is a complete uproar!

So here's to the holidays, wild and bright,
To dreams wrapped in laughter, pure delight.
With mishaps and giggles, our hearts take flight,
As we cherish the moments wrapped in light.

Soft Lullabies of Winter Nights

As snowflakes dance and swirl in flight,
I cuddle up, it's warm and tight.
The blankets stack, a fluffy mound,
With three dogs snoring, what a sound!

The cold wind howls, it tries to creep,
But I'm too cozy, time for sleep.
A cup of cocoa, oh what bliss,
Winter nights promise more than this!

My heater pops, a song so sweet,
While icicles gather at my feet.
The frost outside can't steal my cheer,
For in this warmth, I've nothing to fear!

And thus I dream of springtime hoedowns,
While winter cries and wears its frowns.
Soft lullabies of chilly nights,
Make cozy tales of snowy sights!

Christmas Lights and Candle Flames

The tree is lit, a garish sight,
With blinking bulbs that shout, "Good Night!"
I trip on tinsel, take a fall,
While kids are laughing through it all.

The candle's flame flickers with glee,
Probably laughing at poor me.
Eggnog spills—oh, what a mess!
Yet cookies vanish, I must confess.

The ornaments hang like disco balls,
While Uncle Bob just begins to brawl.
'Tis the season of festive fray,
But let's hope no one runs away!

With laughter loud and spirits bright,
We dance beneath our Christmas lights.
Raise a glass for all to see,
Next year, I'll buy a tree from thee!

Enchanted by the Choir's Hymns

The choir sings with all their might,
Each note takes off like a kite.
I hum along, pretend I'm grand,
But the key is out, they understand.

The organ's booming like a train,
While one poor soul forgets their refrain.
A cat sneaks in, steals the show,
And struts around like he's in a flow.

The choir's robes, each color bright,
Would make a rainbow call for flight.
As voices clash like pots and pans,
With laughter spreading 'cross the lands.

Yet somehow, faith fills the room,
Even when it smells like some old broom.
So here I sit, enchanted, free,
In this chorus of silliness and glee!

The Gift of Yuletide Warmth

The fireside cracks, the logs they pop,
I think I'm good, so I won't stop.
Hot cocoa flows like river streams,
While marshmallows dance in my dreams.

A knitted scarf, two sizes too wide,
Did grandma say, "Look, I tried!"
I wear it proud, though it chokes my neck,
Fashion statements, what the heck?

With every gift, a funny tale,
Like mismatched socks that traverse the pale.
We laugh at sweaters worn with glee,
How did I get this ugly spree?

So let the warmth embrace your heart,
And cherish every silly part.
For in the end, it's laughter's cheer,
That makes Yuletide the best time of year!

Stars Among the Snowflakes

Twinkling lights above us gleam,
Catching snowflakes in a dream.
Falling softly, oh so bright,
Wishing on them every night.

Snowmen wear their hats askew,
Sipping cocoa, just for two.
With each sip, we laugh and play,
Making snowballs every day.

Underneath the moonlit glow,
Outrageous snowball fights will show.
As we tumble down the hill,
Rolling, laughing—what a thrill!

So grab your gear and join the fun,
In winter's snow, we'll never run.
With stars above and snowflakes swirled,
Let's embrace this winter world!

Mistletoe Kisses and Candlelight Wishes

Underneath the mistletoe,
A lovebird's blush, a stolen show.
Lips collide in a splashing thrill,
As giggles dance upon the sill.

Candles flicker, shadows play,
Wishes float, they're here to stay.
Tinsel sparkles, dreams ignite,
Whispered secrets on a night so bright.

Each kiss is wrapped in cocoa cheer,
Warm and fuzzy, oh so near.
Forgot the list, what did I want?
Just a jolly, silly jaunt!

Mismatched socks and hats askew,
Laughter rings while we pursue.
In the glow of candlelight,
Mistletoe magic feels just right!

The Magic of Glittering Nights

Glitter dances on the snow,
Sprinkled sparkles, steal the show.
Fairy lights twinkle like stars,
As laughter travels near and far.

Gathering 'round the fire's glow,
Stories shared with hearts aglow.
S'mores are burnt but spirits high,
As marshmallows go flying by!

Sleepy eyes and yawns galore,
Chasing dreams, oh, what a score!
With every star that makes a wish,
We toast to nights we'll never miss.

So grab a cup of cheer tonight,
And join the magic, pure delight.
We'll dance till dawn in cozy light,
With glittering dreams and hearts so bright!

Sweet Aromas of Cinnamon and Cheer

Cinnamon twirls in the air,
Baking goodies, love to share.
Mixing sugar, flour, and spice,
Christmas cookies—oh, so nice!

The oven hums a cheerful tune,
As gingerbread men start to croon.
Frosting rivers, sprinkles galore,
Tasty treasures that we adore!

Catching scents of pine and zest,
Cozy fires—a warm, sweet nest.
With every whiff, our hearts grow bright,
Gather 'round for pure delight.

So grab a cookie off the plate,
Savor moments, just don't wait.
In the aroma, love draws near,
Sparking joy and holiday cheer!

A Tapestry of Warmth and Wonder

In a world of socks, mismatched and bright,
A lion found courage on a candy's delight.
He danced with the penguins, both bold and bizarre,
While dreaming of fish that could swim from afar.

A turtle in glasses was knitting a hat,
He thought it was warm, but it looked like a cat.
His friends all just giggled, they couldn't refrain,
As the hats became blankets for naps in the rain.

An owl wore a scarf, so fluffy and grand,
While telling his friends of the plans in his band.
They'd sing silly songs about jellybean skies,
And laugh as they spotted a pair of pink flies.

So gather your friends, let the laughter expand,
With a tapestry woven by love's happy hand.
For wonder is found in the quirkiest things,
Like turtles and owls who embrace what life brings.

The Glow of Candles and Hearts

A candle once whispered, 'I'm brighter than most!'
While dreaming of being a soft buttered toast.
It flickered and giggled, danced on the shelf,
'I'll shine like a star, just not on myself!'

He met with a heart-shaped balloon in the night,
Who shared that her float was a wonderful sight.
'But darling,' she said, 'with your wax and your flame,
You're melting my heart, oh, isn't that lame?'

Together they plotted a flight to the moon,
Where candles and hearts would sing a sweet tune.
With laughter and joy, they lit up the sky,
While fireflies watched, buzzing happily by.

A friendship was born, both strange and profound,
Between flickers of love, and a heart that is sound.
So light up your candles and float with your heart,
For in this bright dance, we all play a part.

Festive Reflections in the Snow

The snowflakes were falling, each one was unique,
While a squirrel in boots practiced his vogue peek.
He twirled on the ice with a flair that was grand,
Wishing all of his friends could join in his band.

A snowman named Bob wore a hat too tight,
He complained it was giving him quite a fright.
With carrots for buttons and coal for his smile,
He cha-cha'd and boogied for quite a long while.

Two penguins were sliding, they giggled with cheer,
Saying, 'Look at us, we're the coolest right here!'
They tossed snowballs at each other with glee,
While making a snow angel, oh what a sight to see!

So bundle up tight as the snowflakes swirl by,
Join in with the laughter, just let your heart fly.
In festive reflections, joy dances and glows,
In a wintery wonderland, where happiness flows.

Love's Lanterns in the Winter's Night

In a field full of lanterns, aglow with delight,
A cat in pajamas danced under the night.
He twirled and he jumped, pure joy unconfined,
While humbugs and fireflies formed a strange line.

The stars offered tips on how to dance well,
While giggles and whispers rang out with a bell.
A bear in a tutu joined in with a spin,
Proclaiming, 'Oh, darling, let's all join in!'

The moon blushed and beamed as he watched from above,

While lanterns all flickered, entwined with pure love.
Balloons filled with laughter floated here and there,
As all of the critters forgot every care.

So celebrate love when the winter's so bright,
With lanterns a-glimmering in magical flight.
Together we shine, from our hearts to the night,
In a dance full of wonder, our spirits take flight.

A Symphony of Holiday Laughter

The turkey danced across the floor,
While grandma shouted, "Get back, you bore!"
The carols played off-key and loud,
We laughed so hard, we scared the crowd.

The cookies burned, but who would care?
We tossed them high and made a glare!
The fruitcake rolled, it made a run,
But even that was still more fun.

The lights flickered like a jazz band,
Singing bright tunes across the land.
Our holiday feast was quite a sight,
With every bite, we took in delight!

So here's to laughter, bright and bold,
In every tale that's ever told.
May every holiday, near or far,
Bring joy to all, like a shining star.

Underneath the Starlit Sky

We set up camp and pitched our tent,
But found we'd brought no food, not a cent!
The stars looked down, they twinkled bright,
While we flipped a coin for a midnight bite.

A raccoon joined in our late-night feast,
He grabbed our snacks like a little beast!
We laughed and shared, an odd delight,
Underneath the stars, so vivid and bright.

Our flashlight flickered, went dark with a pop,
We fumbled around till we heard a plop!
The cooler spilled, a funny mess,
"Is this camping?" we surely guessed!

So here we sit, no gourmet stars,
Just nature's snacks from old candy bars.
Underneath the starlit sky we find,
That laughter's the best view, oh so kind!

The Glow of Love in Every Corner

The lights went up with a sudden snap,
A flash like magic, or perhaps a trap!
We tangled bulbs, and laughed till we cried,
Love glowed brighter, even if the lights died.

The cats spun 'round in holiday cheer,
Chasing ribbons that vanished near.
Each corner shone with delight so clear,
As family joined from far and near.

"Are we festive or just confused?"
Each ornament that broke, we simply used!
With laughter and love, we saved the night,
The glow of joy was our true light.

In every corner hangs a cherished tale,
From granddad's jokes to mom's funny fail.
The warmth of love, it makes us whole,
Lighting up every heart and soul.

Cherished Moments Wrapped in Light

The wrapping paper flew with a zest,
Each gift revealed was simply the best!
A sweater two sizes too small indeed,
But the laughter it sparked was all we'd need.

We had papers crumpled like zany art,
Mixed with giggles that warmed the heart.
Cards forgotten, tossed to the side,
Yet cherished memories still abide.

A puppy barked with a jolly grin,
He unwrapped joy, let the fun begin!
With every chuckle, the room filled bright,
Cherished moments wrapped in pure light.

So here's to the folly, the fun, and delight,
In every surprise that makes spirits bright.
We'll treasure these times, through thick and thin,
For laughter and love are where we begin.

Glittering Ornaments and Sweet Goodness

On the tree, the ornaments gleam,
Hiding candy canes that dream.
But who stole the cookies, oh what a shame,
Can't point fingers; they're all to blame!

Tinsel's tangled, a shimmering mess,
Lights flashing like we're in a stress.
The cat's found a way to leap and play,
Now it's a tree-tastrophe on this festive day!

Eggnog spills on the sequined dress,
Uncle Bob claims it's a holiday bless.
While Grandma's baking her holiday cake,
Adds too much salt, for goodness' sake!

Yet laughter fills the rooms with cheer,
Even if ornaments disappear.
With glitter, sweets, and silly fun,
This holiday's quirky, but it's the best one!

Shadows Dancing by the Firelight

In the corner, shadows start to play,
A limbo dance, what a sight today!
The cat's in the spotlight, tail all a-fluff,
She's the nocturnal diva, but can't get enough!

S'mores are melting, a gooey delight,
I dropped mine again, what a messy plight.
The marshmallow's stuck to my favorite shirt,
This fire's my friend, but it's got some hurt!

Ghost stories are told with a jump and a scare,
While someone's laughing, forgetting their chair.
A plop on the floor, as laughter erupts,
A haunting, perhaps? Or just some hiccuped?

Yet in the shadows, we all find our light,
Dancing around with faces so bright.
With laughter and love, we'll hold steady tight,
In memories glowing, forever in sight!

Cloaked in Radiance of Season's Greetings

Wrapped in layers, I can't find my feet,
With scarves and mittens, it's quite the feat.
Out in the snow, I'm lost in my gear,
Search for the path, but it disappears!

Snowflakes twirling like they're on a spree,
Dancing around, just trying to be free.
But down goes my nose in the winter's embrace,
A frost-bitten grin takes over my face!

Neighbors shout joys wrapped in bright lights,
While I'm just hoping my house can ignite.
Caught in the glare of bright glowing trees,
I step on a twig — oh, someone, please!

Yet cheer fills the air with a whimsical tune,
As laughter erupts, we all sing with swoon.
Cloaked in the spirit, we're all warm tonight,
With the joy of the season burning so bright!

Whirling Snowflakes and Laughter's Ring

Whirling snowflakes, they dance and twirl,
Catch one on your tongue, give it a whirl.
But slippery sidewalks ruin my glide,
A winter ballet, but I'm taking a ride!

Bundled up tight, I venture outside,
Building a snowman, it's wintertime pride.
Carrot for a nose, his smile is wide,
Until the sun shines, and he takes a slide!

Laughter rings out from every direction,
Snowball fights lead to grand confection.
"Dodge this!" they scream in a wild delight,
While my aim's more like a snowflake in flight!

The evening wraps up with cheeks all aglow,
Hot cocoa waiting, stealing the show.
With whirling snowflakes and joy ever near,
What a great season, to hold dear!

Unity in the Glow of Firelight

In the circle, we all sit tight,
S'mores in hand, what a delight!
But one misfires, oh what a mess,
Chocolate on eyebrows, we just can't guess.

The flames dance high, a wild ballet,
Our laughter echoes, night turns to day.
Who knew sparks could fly like this?
Even the marshmallow won't be missed!

We tell ghost stories, but roast a few,
Each scary tale, a laugh in lieu.
Huddled close, we share the heat,
And forged in fire, we can't be beat!

As embers glow and shadows creep,
We promise not to fall asleep.
For in this warmth, our hearts align,
Together forever, like toast with wine!

Echoes of Joy in Frosty Air

Snowflakes falling, soft and white,
We slip and slide, what a sight!
Laughter rises, a joyful cheer,
Hot cocoa waits, it's finally here!

Snowmen stand, with carrot nose,
But they start melting, everyone knows.
"Quick, take a photo!" we all shout,
Before he becomes just water spout!

We build a fort, a snowy mound,
"Take that!" we scream, snowballs abound!
But then we trip, fall in a heap,
And roll away, in laughter deep.

As the sun sets, we head inside,
Warmed by fun, that can't subside.
Echoes linger in frosty air,
Friendship grows, beyond compare!

The Spirit of Togetherness

In the kitchen, we all convene,
Chopping onions makes us keen.
But who's the one adding salt by the pound?
Dinner's a laugh fest, all around!

The chaos stirs, pots clatter loud,
"Is that a recipe?" we all crowd.
But recipes ditch us, we just ignore,
Stirring and flipping, who needs a chore?

When the table is set, it's a feast,
Even if the cakes have gone yeast!
Wit and humor fill the room,
As we munch and laugh, dispelling gloom.

With every bite, our spirits lift,
Joy is the heart's greatest gift.
In this kitchen, love's the key,
Togetherness wraps us like a warm tea!

Serendipity in the Snow

Woke up to white, oh what a shock!
Lost my shoe, tripped on a rock.
Serendipity strikes, or is it luck?
Finding a snowball, oh what a pluck!

We wander out, bundled and snug,
But end up tangled in one big hug.
Snowflakes melting on our nose,
We giggle like kids, that's how it goes!

A snowball fight turns into a race,
Each frozen flake, a friendly embrace.
Chasing laughter as the sun starts to set,
Serendipitous moments, we won't forget!

As darkness drops, we head back home,
With icy toes, we sit and roam.
Fireside tales, our hearts aglow,
It's the magic of snow, our spirits flow!

A Journey into Winter's Heart

Snowflakes dance like it's a ball,
They cover rooftops, trees, and all.
A chilly breeze finds each cold spot,
Yet hot cocoa hits the right spot.

My nose is red, my toes are cold,
I wear ten layers, so I'm told.
The snowman smiles with stick arms wide,
He can't move, but still has pride.

Winter's here with frosty air,
With sledding hills and laughs to share.
We'll skate on ponds, but with a twist,
'Til I slip and fall, and cannot resist.

Yet in this freeze, we hold so dear,
The warmth of friends and holiday cheer.
For though it's cold, we bring the fun,
A journey through winter's heart begun.

The Miracles of Starlit Nights

Stars above, like tiny lights,
Twinkle down on winter nights.
I gaze up high, a wish in mind,
For socks that match, oh how unkind!

The moon hangs low, it's quite a sight,
Like a giant lamp, glowing bright.
My hat is crooked, my scarf's too tight,
But who cares? I'm a star tonight!

Snowball fights break out with glee,
I throw and miss, oh woe is me!
But laughter fills the chilly air,
As winter's magic is everywhere.

So raise a cup and toast this dream,
For starlit nights, we're on a team.
With friends beside, it feels just right,
In joy we bask on winter nights.

Frosty Kisses and Sweet Greetings

Frosty kisses from old man Winter,
Leave my cheeks rosy, I can't help but splinter.
Each breath I puff turns into mist,
Who knew cold air could feel like bliss?

Jingle bells ring at every turn,
In snowball fights, we gladly learn.
But watch your back! A snowball flies,
Right in the ear, oh what a surprise!

Hot chocolate warms my freezing hands,
As snowflakes land on my new, bright bands.
Marshmallows float, they dance and swirl,
In my cup, it's a winter world.

So here's to frosty, silly fun,
With snowflakes falling, the day's not done.
Sweet greetings spread and laughter loudly sings,
In the chill, it's joy that winter brings.

Hopes Kindled by Flickering Lights

Flickering lights on trees shine bright,
They blink and twinkle with pure delight.
I trip on cords, but never mind,
The magic's more than you can find.

Neighbors gather with cookies to share,
A pie for a singing voice that's rare.
And who knew Aunt Mary could really bake?
Wait, is that fruitcake? Oh, for goodness' sake!

Hopes around us begin to glow,
As laughter spreads, and warmth does flow.
With carolers singing all through the night,
Their voices lift us, a wonderful sight.

So cherish the moments, the love in sight,
As we huddle close, it feels so right.
For in the glow of the lights so fair,
We find our hopes, beyond compare.

Milton Keynes UK
Ingram Content Group UK Ltd.
UKHW021420081224
452166UK00007B/55